PARTS OF THE BODY

INFO PICS

BY HARRIET BRUNDLE

BookLife PUBLISHING

©2020
BookLife Publishing Ltd.
King's Lynn
Norfolk PE30 4LS

All rights reserved.
Printed in Malaysia.

A catalogue record for this book is available from the British Library.

ISBN: 978-1-83927-048-2

Written by:
Harriet Brundle

Edited by:
Madeline Tyler

Designed by:
Drue Rintoul

All facts, statistics, web addresses and URLs in this book were verified as valid and accurate at time of writing. No responsibility for any changes to external websites or references can be accepted by either the author or publisher.

NOTTINGHAMSHIRE EDUCATION LIBRARY SERVICE	
E220206950	
Askews & Holts	20-Jan-2021
612	

Image Credits

Cover & Throughout – K-Nick, movinglines.studio, MicroOne, Andy Frith, Anatolir, Macrovector, InshStyle, Maksim, EgudinKa, logistock. 2&3 – SeamlessPatterns. 4&5 – Annasunny24, VVadyab Pico. 6–9 – Sudowoodo, atabik yusuf djufni, Kilroy79, Panda Vector, Tetiana Yurchenko, Fagreia. 10&11 – Macrovector, Sonechko57. 12&13 – Macrovector, Sonechko57, VitalasArt, ArtVarStudio. 14&15 – kckate16, Photoroyalty, hvostikw. 16&17 – nekoztudio, Tribalium, DRogatnev, LDarin. 18–21 – HappyPictures, VectorMine, metamorworks, webreg30380. 22&23 – MTVector, vectortatu, LOVE YOU, Rvector, Wor Sang Jun, VectorPlotnikoff, Paper Teo. All images courtesy of Shutterstock.com. With thanks to Getty Images, Thinkstock Photo and iStockphoto.

CONTENTS

Page 4   Your Body
Page 6   Body Parts
Page 10 Organs
Page 14 Skin, Hair and Nails
Page 16 Blood
Page 18 The Body Systems
Page 22 Taking Care of Your Body Parts
Page 24 Glossary and Index

Words that look like this can be found in the glossary on page 24.

YOUR BODY

Although we all look different, many of us have the same body parts.

Your body is constantly moving, changing and growing.

Make sure you do enough exercise.

Look after your personal hygiene by doing these things:
- Have a bath or shower every day
- Clean your teeth twice every day
- Wash your hands after you've been to the toilet

GLOSSARY

blood vessels	tubes in the body that blood flows through
clot	a lump of thick, sticky blood
diet	the kinds of food that a person or animal usually eats
filter	remove unwanted materials by passing through something, such as a sieve
functions	works properly
nerves	bundles of little fibres that carry information around the body
nutrients	natural substances that plants and animals need in order to grow and stay healthy
oxygen	a natural gas that living things need in order to survive
personal hygiene	being clean and healthy
temperature	how hot or cold something is
tissue	groups of cells that are like each other and do the same job
unique	unlike anything or anyone else
waste	things left over that are no longer needed

INDEX

bones 8
brain 13, 18
cells 9, 16–17
food 12, 20
heart 10, 16, 19

kidneys 12, 21
lungs 11, 20
protection 14–15, 19
skeleton 8–9
stomach 12, 20

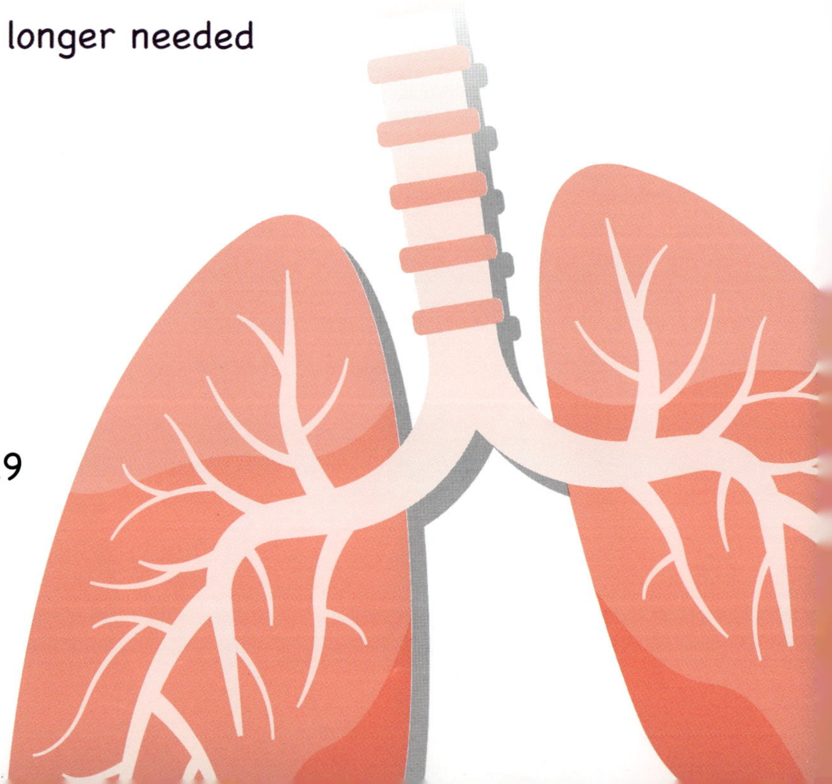

TAKING CARE OF YOUR BODY PARTS

It's important to look after your body and give it the things it needs to stay healthy.

Try to eat a healthy <u>diet</u>.

Don't forget to drink plenty of water.

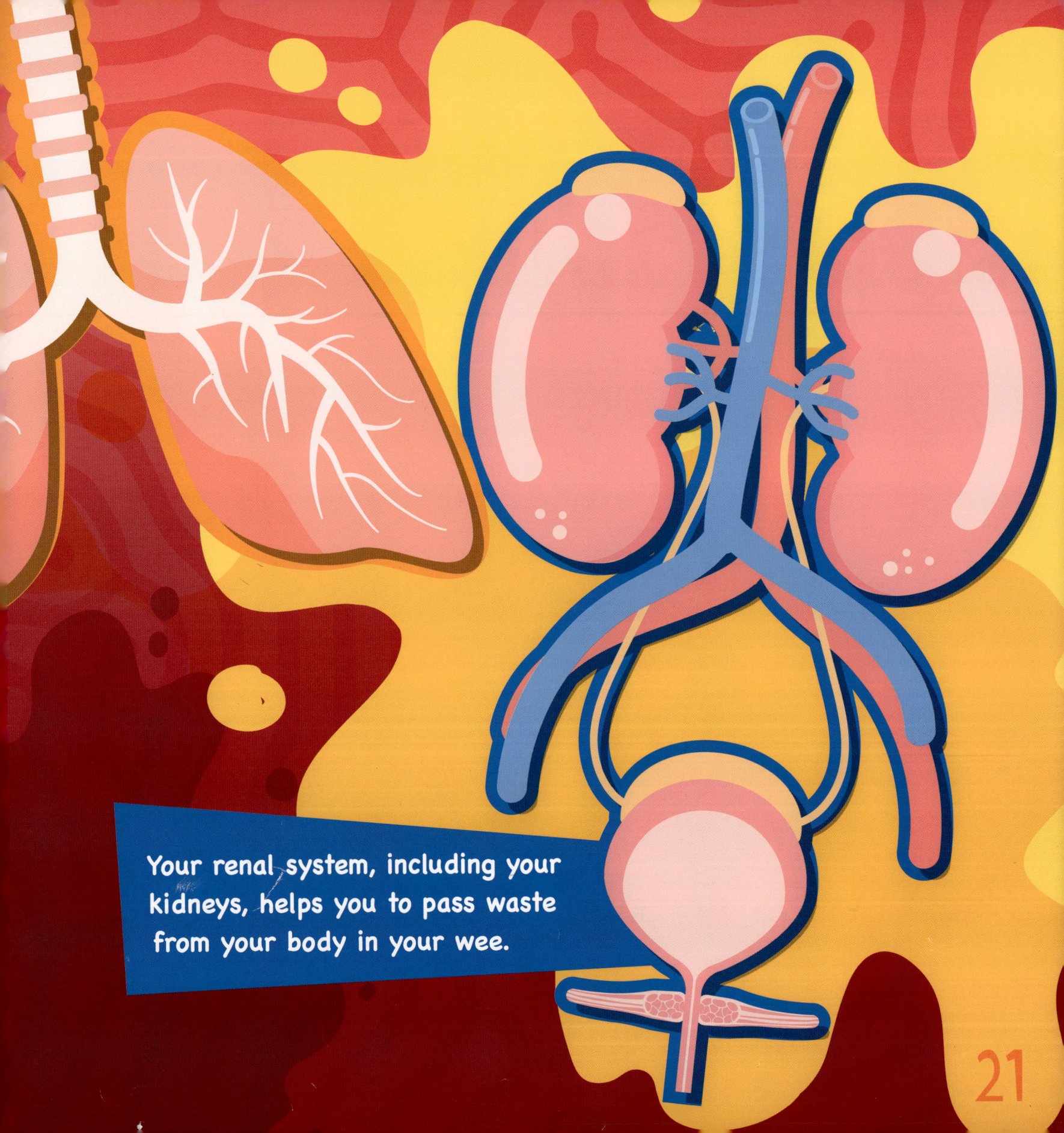

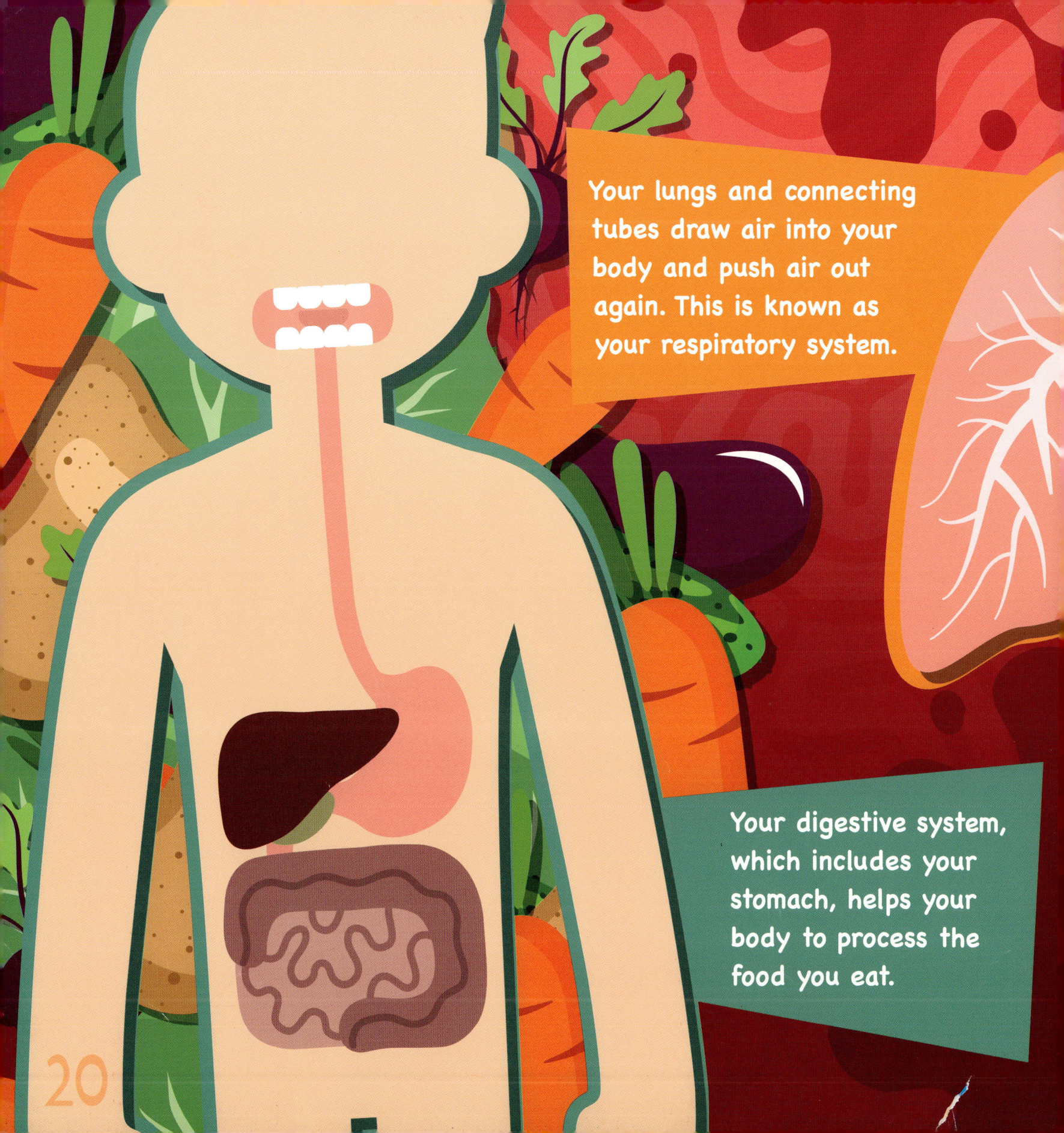

Your lungs and connecting tubes draw air into your body and push air out again. This is known as your respiratory system.

Your digestive system, which includes your stomach, helps your body to process the food you eat.

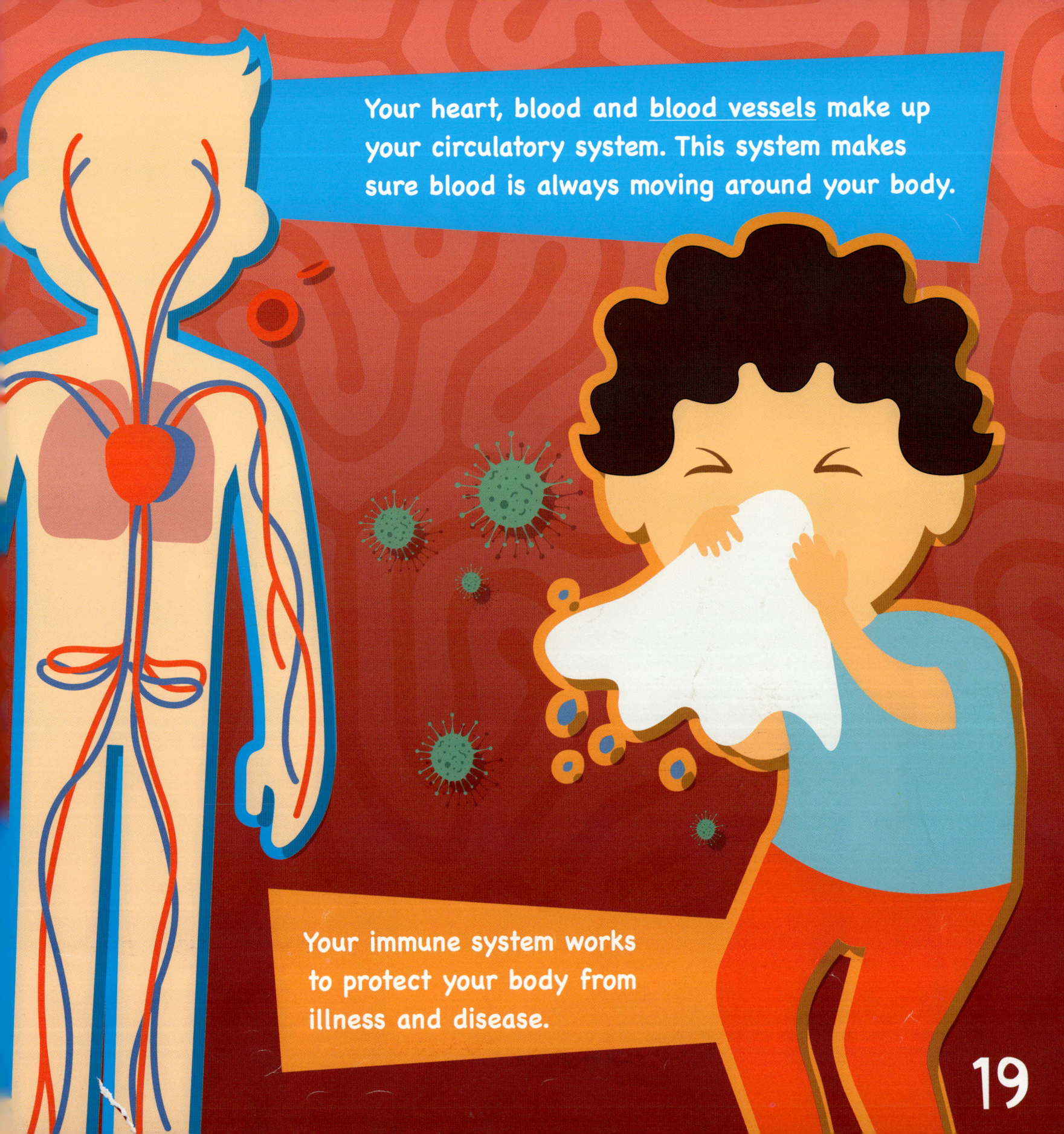

Your heart, blood and <u>blood vessels</u> make up your circulatory system. This system makes sure blood is always moving around your body.

Your immune system works to protect your body from illness and disease.

THE BODY SYSTEMS

Within your body, different parts work together in teams to form body systems.

Your brain and <u>nerves</u> form your nervous system. This system carries messages to your brain and to the different parts of your body.

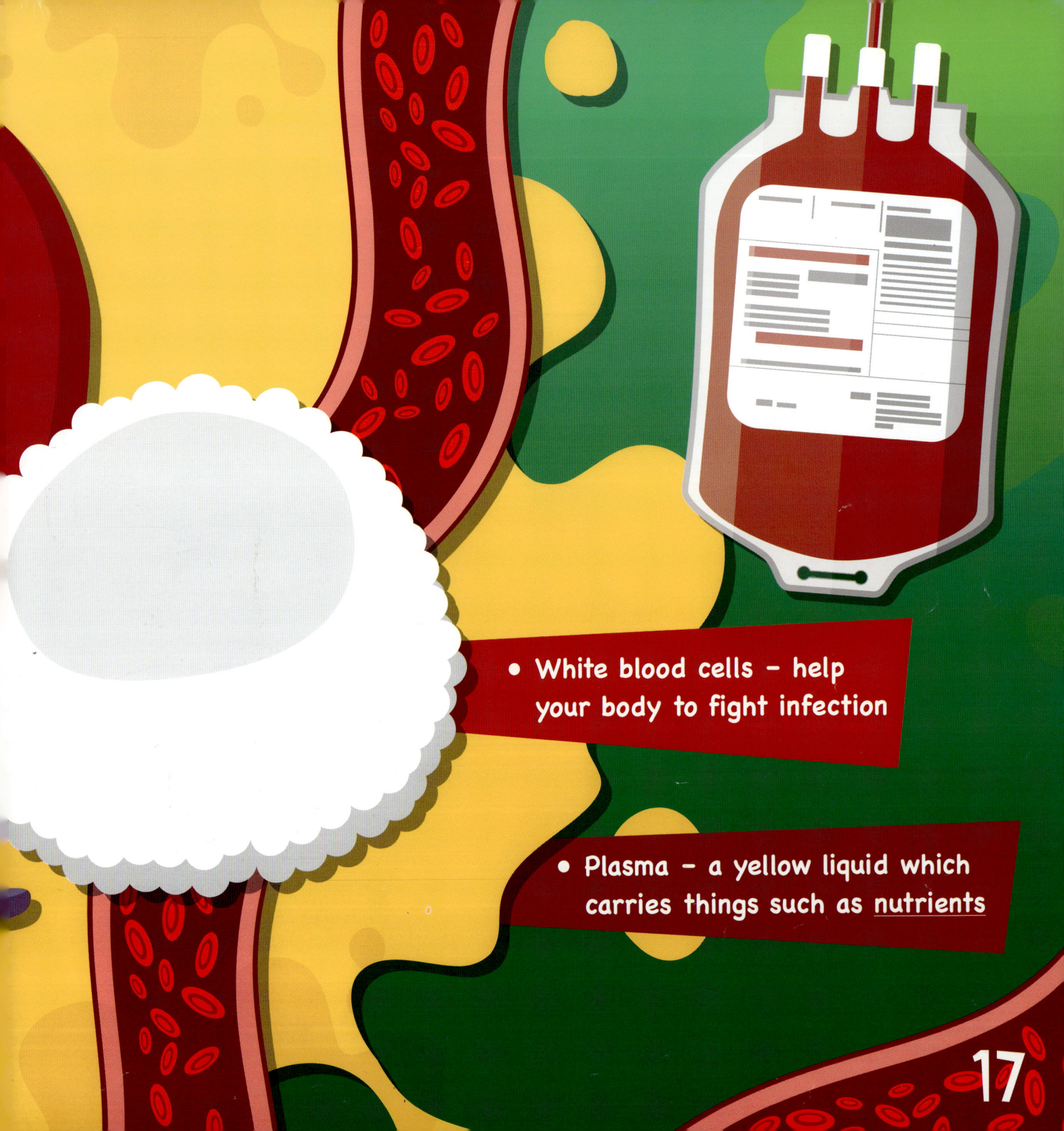

- White blood cells – help your body to fight infection

- Plasma – a yellow liquid which carries things such as nutrients

BLOOD

With every heartbeat, blood is pumped around your body.

Blood is made up of:

- Red blood cells – carry oxygen around your body

- Platelets – help your blood to clot

Hair helps to keep you warm. Some of your hairs help to protect your body parts. For example, your eyelashes help to stop dust getting in your eyes.

Nails protect the ends of your fingers and toes. They help you to scratch and to pick things up.

SKIN, HAIR AND NAILS

Skin is the largest organ in the human body.

Skin protects your body, helps you control your <u>temperature</u> and allows you to feel things such as heat.

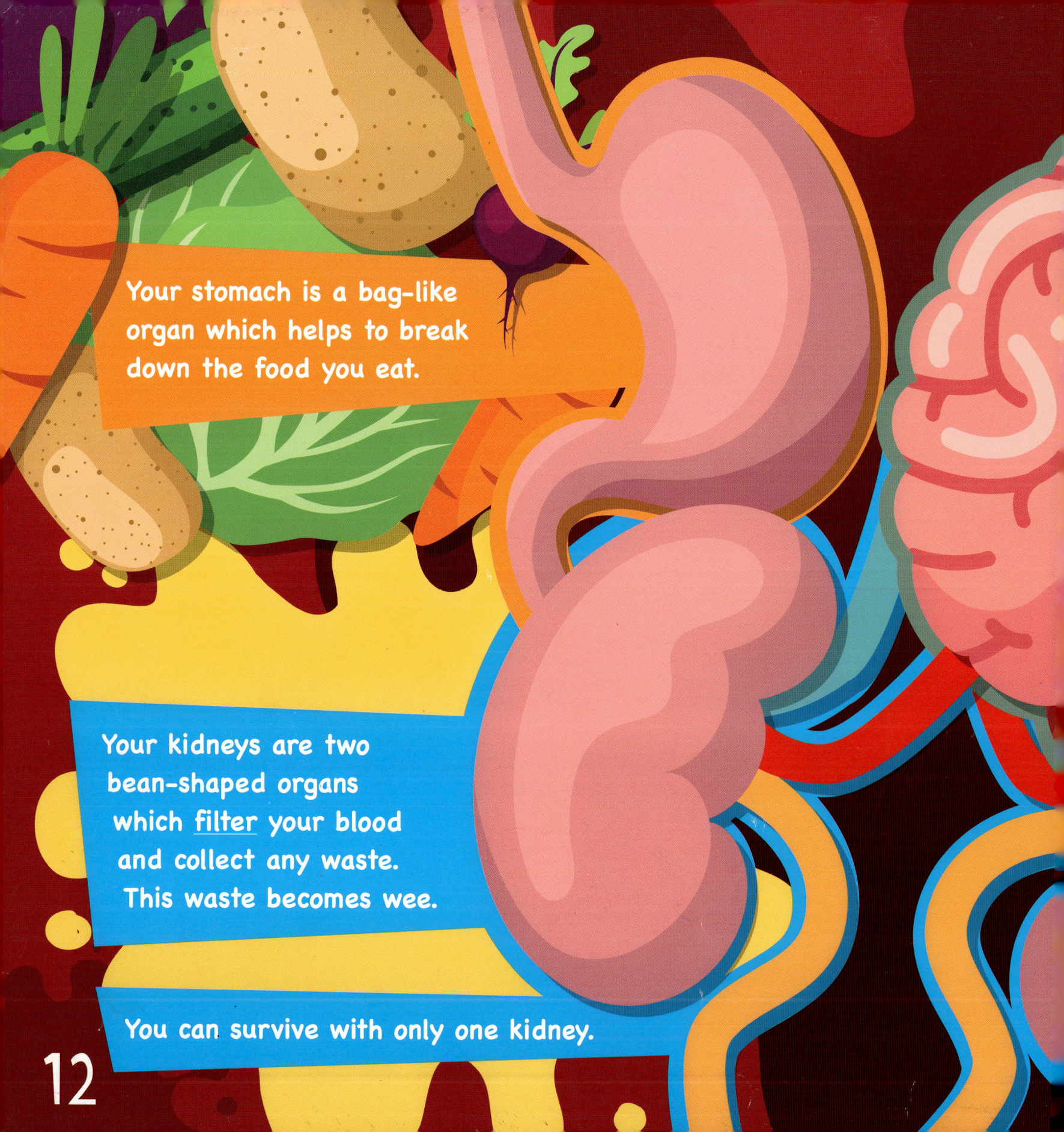

Your stomach is a bag-like organ which helps to break down the food you eat.

Your kidneys are two bean-shaped organs which <u>filter</u> your blood and collect any waste. This waste becomes wee.

You can survive with only one kidney.

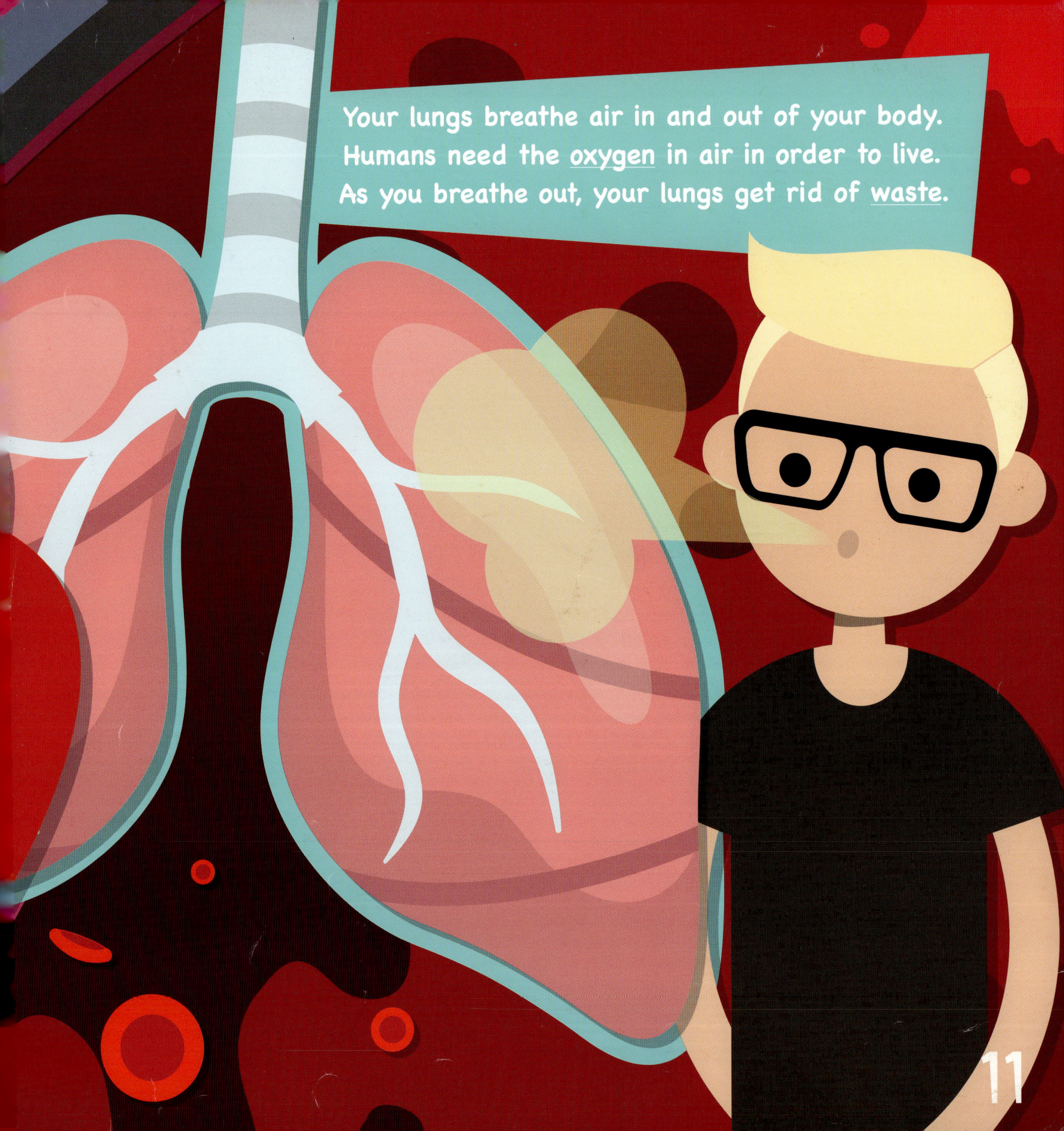

ORGANS

Organs are parts of the body that have a very particular function. These are just some of the body's organs.

Your heart pumps blood around the body. Your heart is around the size of your fist and it works day and night throughout your whole life.

Your heart pumps more than five litres of blood every minute.

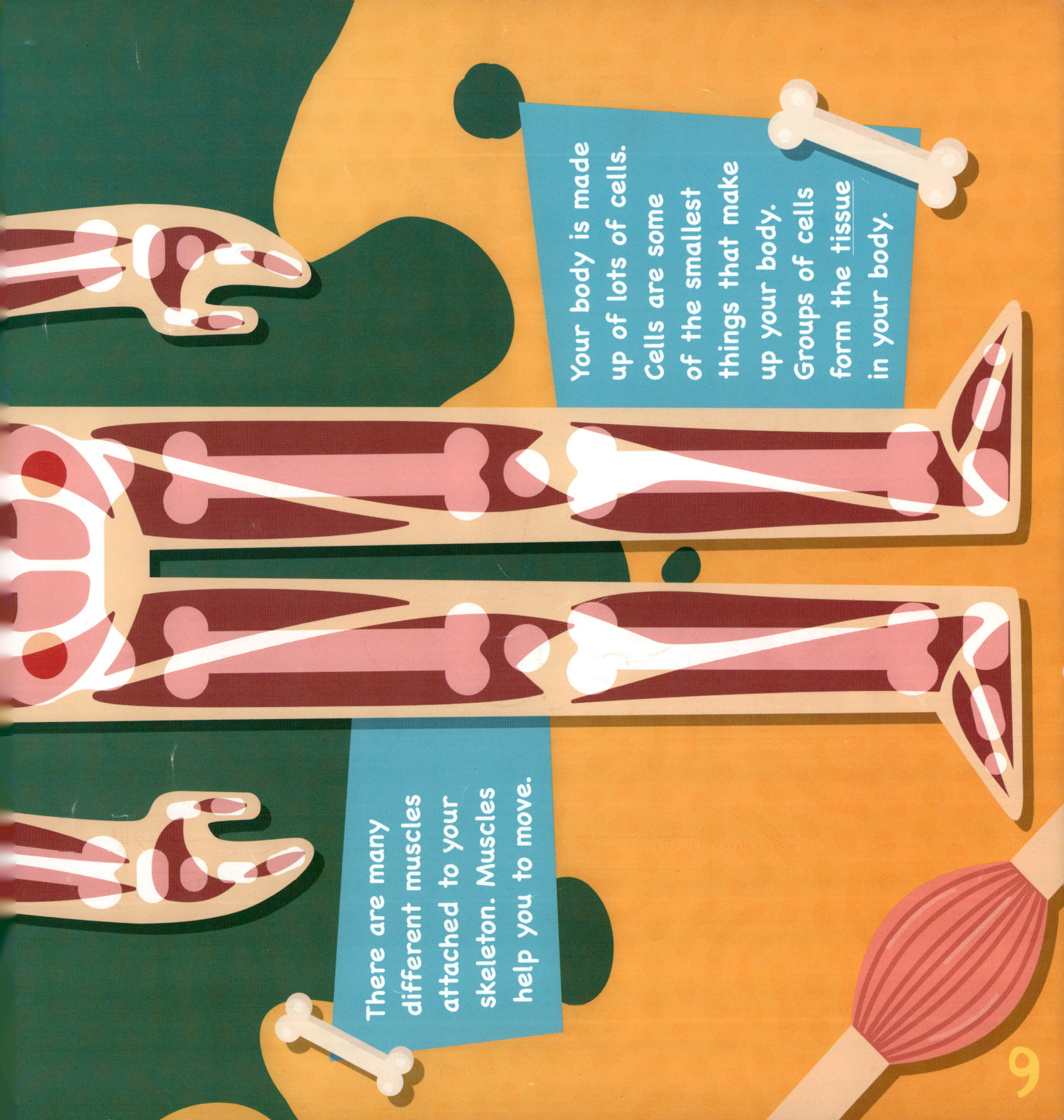

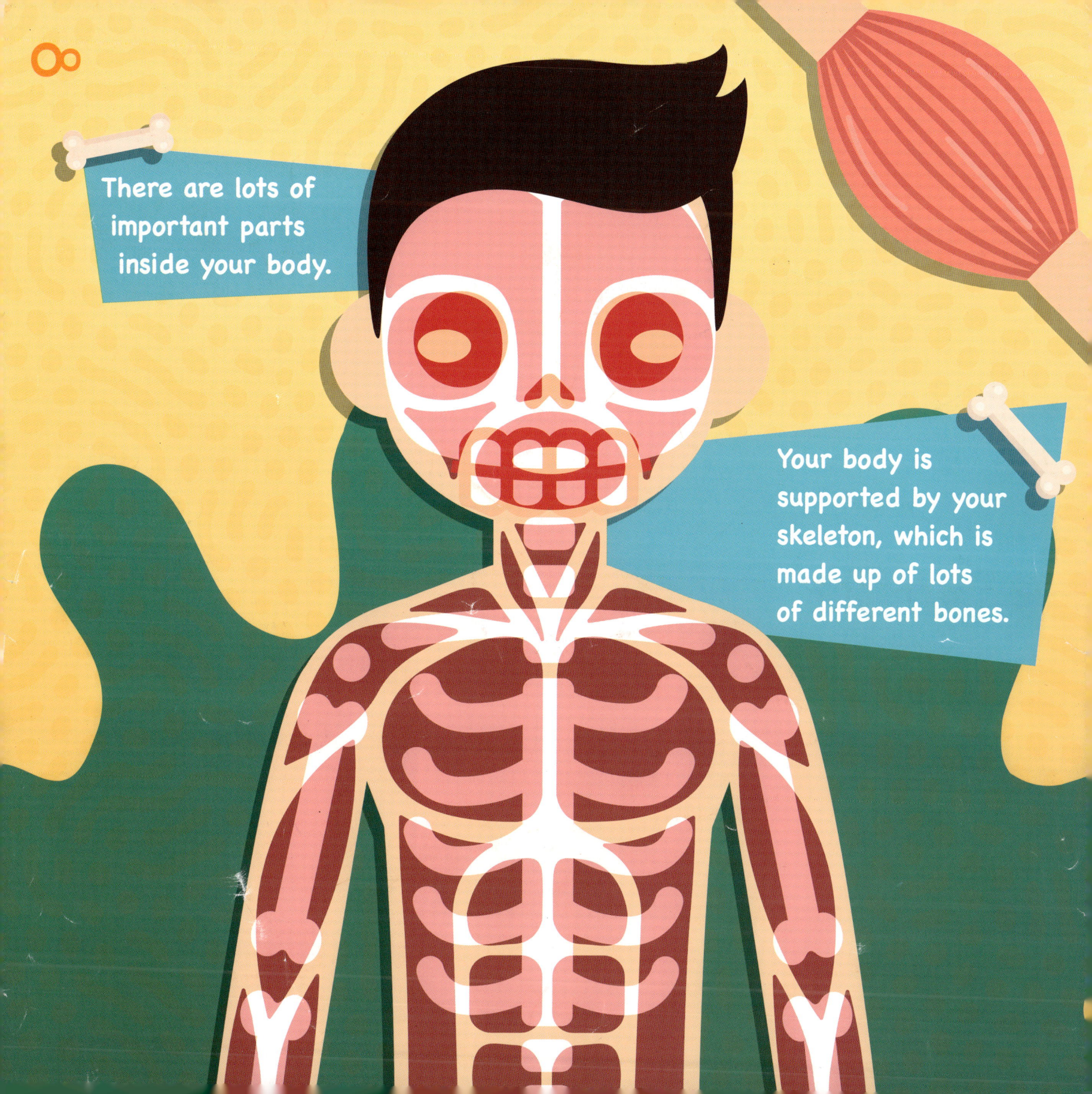

BODY PARTS

These are some of your outside body parts. Each has its own job to do, as well as working together with other parts.

- Head
- Ear
- Eye
- Nose
- Mouth
- Neck
- Shoulder
- Arm

As you move through life from being a baby to old age, your body will change in how it looks and how it functions.

Each of your body parts has a particular job. Some are important for keeping you alive.